People in art

OXFORD
PRIMARY
art

Norman Binch

Portraits

These pictures show us some of the different ways in which artists have made portraits.

Can you see some of the differences?

The Egyptian portrait is over 3000 years old and is a *relief carving*. It is really quite flat but is carved so that the light makes the figure stand out from the background. The Egyptians carved heads mostly in profile – from the side.

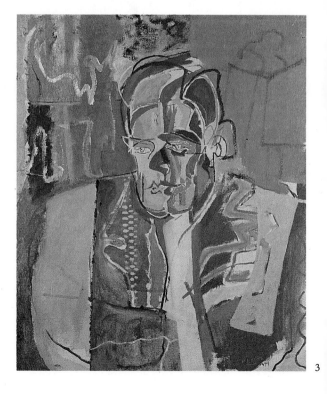

2

1

3

The drawing by Rubens is very *realistic* but the two oil paintings are not. Why do you think the artists painted them in this way? Can you say what makes the photograph so dramatic?

5

4

1. Egyptian relief carving of Rameses II as a child. 19th Dynasty, 1290-1224 BC

2. Paul Cezanne (1839-1906). Young girl with a doll, 1902-4

3. Patrick Heron, Portrait of T S Eliot, 1949

4. Peter Paul Rubens (1577-1640). Lady in waiting to the Infanta Isabella

5. Angus McBean, Portrait of Vivien Leigh, 1952

Faces

If you look carefully at these faces you can learn a lot about portraiture.

For example, what can you tell about the mood of the subjects – how they might be feeling?

What creates the mood? Is it the eyes, or is it the whole expression on the face? How has Memling created the feeling of calmness in his portrait of a woman?

Look at the different ways of drawing hair, and details such as wrinkles and folds in the skin to show age.

Can you see where the light is coming from in the portraits of the two men?

1. Hans Memling (c.1435/40-1495). Woman's portrait

2. Lucien Freud. Portrait of Francis Bacon, 1952

3. Albrecht Durer (1471-1528). Portrait of the artist's mother, 1514

4. Giovanni Bellini (c.1430-1516). Portrait of man with a turban

1

2

3

4

Heads

Sometimes artists make heads rather than portraits to say something about people in general. Are these portraits of people or are they heads which represent people in gesseal?

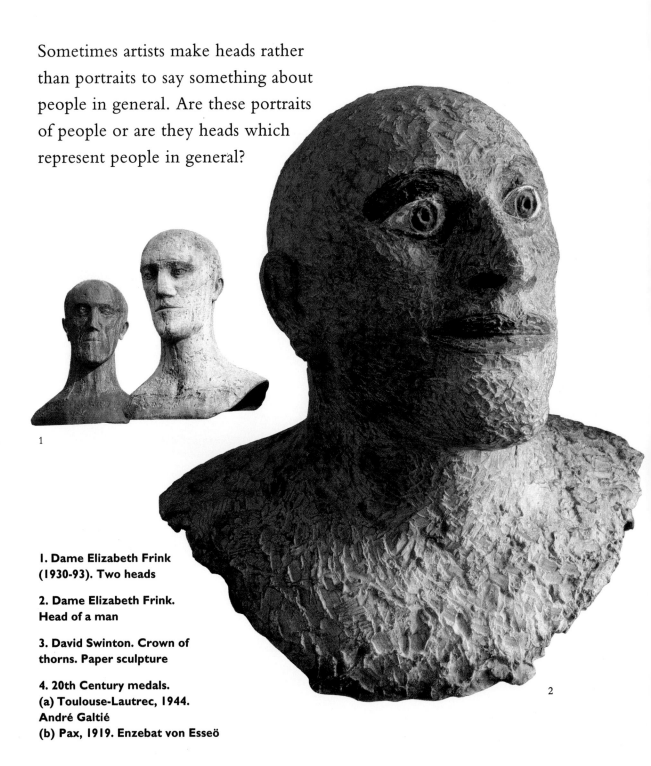

1. Dame Elizabeth Frink (1930-93). Two heads

2. Dame Elizabeth Frink. Head of a man

3. David Swinton. Crown of thorns. Paper sculpture

4. 20th Century medals.
(a) Toulouse-Lautrec, 1944. André Galtié
(b) Pax, 1919. Enzebat von Esseö

Heads are used on medals and stamps to commemorate people or events. These heads would have been modelled in wax and then cast in bronze.

The head of Christ is made from paper.

4a

4b

3

Religious figures

People in many religions make images of their gods and religious leaders. Here, there are two stone carvings of Buddha, a wooden figure of Dewi Sri, the rice goddess, and another stone carving of Indra. Indra is the ancient Hindu god of the heavens, who is usually represented riding on an elephant.

1

What does the word 'scale' mean? Look at the two pictures below. Can you see the difference in scale?

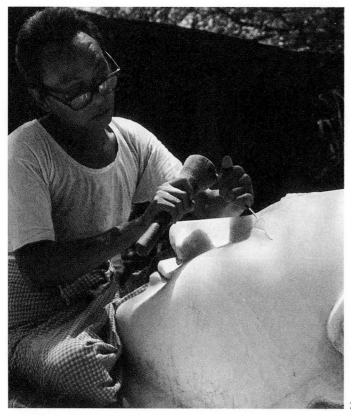
2

3

1. Head of Buddha, carved in grey schist. 3/4th Century BC

2. Carving a statue of Buddha. Pagan, Indonesia

3. Dewi Sri, rice goddess, being painted. Bali, Indonesia

4. Indra. Eastern Ganga period, 11th Century

4

Christian carvings

These are stone carvings of Christian themes. The medieval carvings of the kings bringing gifts to the infant Jesus and the 'Flight out of Egypt' are from France, but you see many similar carvings in English churches. The carving of the Madonna and Child was done over 300 years later in the 'Renaissance' period. (Renaissance means 'rebirth' – of ancient Greek and Roman art forms)

What differences can you see in the carvings? Look at the details of the faces, hair and drapery. Is the stone the same?

1

2

1. Adoration of the Magi. 12th Century. Autun, France

2. The flight out of Egypt, 12th Century. Autun, France

3. Michelangelo (1475-1564). Madonna and child. 1501. (Detail)

4. Michelangelo. Madonna and child

3

4

Figure drawing and painting

Artists often make many studies of figures before they include them in paintings. These show some of the different materials and techniques they use – pencil, watercolour, chalk, etching and oil paint.

Studies are done to collect information, to try out techniques, and to develop ideas.

Your own sketchbooks might be used to make studies for paintings and for trying out your own ideas.

1

2

3

4

5

1. Rembrandt van Rijn (1606-69). Drunken Lot

2. Michelangelo. 1475-1564. Studies for Libyan Sybil

3. Goya (1746-1828). The Colossus

4. Sir Mathew Smith. Nude, Fitzroy Square No 1, 1916

5. Robert Hills. Studies of country children. c.1815

Families

These are all paintings about families.
Millais' painting is his idea of what
Jesus' early life might have been like
in his father's carpentry shop.

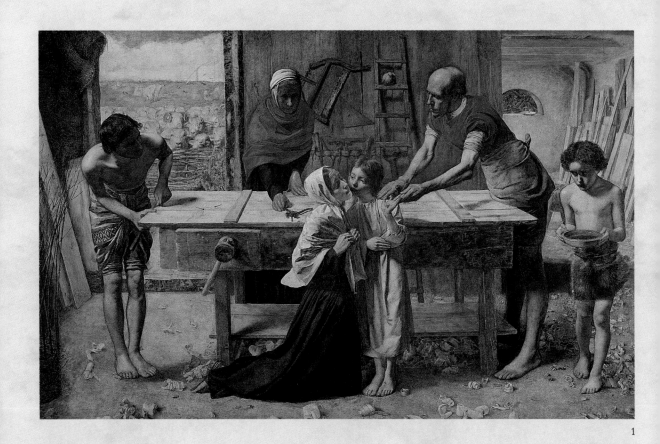

1

How do you think the family feels about 'dad' being on strike in the painting by von Herkomer?

What do you think the other two paintings might be about?

1. John Everett Millais. Christ in the house of his parents. 'The carpenter's shop'. 1849-50

2. Sir Hubert von Herkomer (1849-1941). 'On strike' 1891

3. David Hockney. My parents, 1977

4. George Grosz. A married couple, 1930

2

3

4

People working

These four pictures have things in common. What are they?

When Mary Cassatt made the print of 'The Fitting', women artists didn't have the freedom to go out and paint the same subjects as men, so they tended to paint domestic scenes. Jan Vermeer painted domestic scenes because they were popular with the people who bought his work. Maggie Hambling is a successful contemporary portrait painter. What do you think her subject is doing?

1

2

Why do you think we know so little about women
artists in the past?

4

3

1. Mary Cassatt (1844-1926). The fitting. Print

2. Gluing a paper umbrella onto a frame. Thailand

3. Maggie Hambling. Portrait of Dorothy Hodgkin, 1985

4. Jan Vermeer (1632-75). The lacemaker c.1661

People at play

These illustrations show some of the different sports and pastimes depicted by artists from different times and places. Compare the painting of children boxing from 3000 years ago with the contemporary painting of Viv Richards batting.

1

2

1. Fresco of boxing children. Knossos palace 1500 BC

2. William Bowyer. 'Viv' Richards, 1986

3. Girls performing a Kathal dance. Mughal c.1675

4. Edgar Degas. At the theatre

5. Edgar Degas (1834-1917). Little dancer, aged 14, 1880-81

Look at the differences between the painting of the Kathal Dancers and the drawing and sculpture of Degas.

Can you say how they are different?

4

3

5

19

People at leisure

1

Compare the painting of the 'Luncheon of the Boating Party' with the 'Peasant Tavern'. What differences can you see? Is there a difference between the people in the two paintings? How are they different? What are they doing to enjoy themselves? Can you see how they were painted?

What are the similarities between the painting by Manet and the poster by Ruskin Spear? What are the differences in the backgrounds of the two pictures ?

2

1. Pierre Auguste Renoir (1841-1919). The luncheon of the boating party

2. Adriean van Ostade (1610-84) Peasant tavern

3. Edouard Manet. The bar at the Folies-Bergere, 1882

4. Ruskin Spear. Poster for London Transport, 1988

3

4

On the beach

These are three different paintings of people on the beach. William Orpen's 'On the beach, Howth' would have been painted in the studio from studies done out of doors. The other two were painted in the open air in order to capture the 'impression' of atmosphere and light. The artists were influenced by French 'impressionists' such as Monet.

1

2

Look carefully at the colours used by Philip Wilson Steer. He uses 'complementary' colours which are 'opposites' and create the greatest contrast with each other; orange-blue, green-red, yellow-mauve.

3

1. **James Abbott McNeil Whistler. Beach scene. c.1883**

2. **William Orpen. On the beach, Howth, 1910**

3. **Philip Wilson Steer (1860-1942). Boulogne sands, 1888-91**

People in the circus

The circus is a favourite theme of artists. Clowns came from drama and mime. These illustrations show some of the ways that clowns and acrobats have been depicted. The masks of famous clowns show typical ways in which clowns make up their faces.

3

4

2

1. Masks of famous clowns

2. Georges Rouault
(1871-1958) Clown with
monkey. (Detail)

3. Marino Marini
(1901-80). Horse and
harlequin

4. Marc Chagall
(1887-1985). The circus

People at war

These are some examples of armour which people used to protect themselves in battle. They are beautifully made and very decorative, but also frightening.

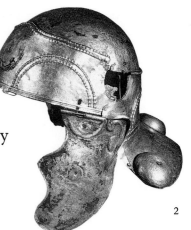

2

1

3

These two paintings are very similar but there are important differences. Make a list of the similarities and a list of the differences and see which is the longer.

4

5

1. Japanese suit of armour, 1748

2. Roman cavalry helmet

3. The Battersea Shield. 1st Century BC

4. Goya. 'The 3rd of May' - execution of the defenders of Madrid

5. Manet. The execution of Emperor Maximilian

Lonely people

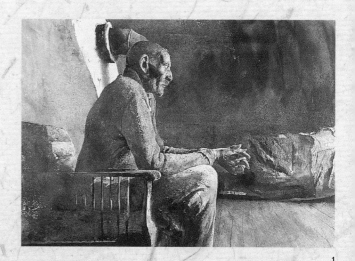

1

What do you feel when you look at these paintings?

Can you imagine what Christina and the old man might be feeling?

2

How does Edward Hopper create the
feeling of loneliness in this painting?

Cindy Sherman takes many photographs
of herself. What can we tell about her
from the photograph?

3

4

1. **Andrew Wyeth (b.1917). An old black man**

2. **Andrew Wyeth. Christina's world**

3. **Edward Hopper. Automat 1927**

4. **Cindy Sherman. Untitled No.96 1981**

Things to do

Portraits and Faces

Make a series of portraits using different materials.

Draw carefully some details such as eyes, noses and ears. Mask parts of your own face and, looking in a mirror, draw what you can see. Try drawing different expressions of just your mouth or eyes.

 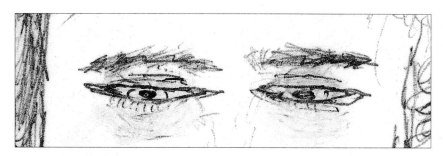

Try modelling some portraits in *relief*.

Now try making some portraits which are not 'realistic' but still tell us what you think the person is like.

Figures

Make a lot of drawings of your friends or family. Use them
to *compose* a painting about them working or playing a game.

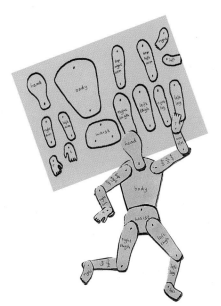

With your friends, make some masks
and make up your faces to become
clowns or other kinds of performers
in the circus.

Words to remember

bronze – a mixture of metals, mainly copper and tin, often used in casting.

casting – using a mould to get an exact copy of an object in another material. Think of using a jelly mould to understand how it works.

'heads' – not portraits of a particular person : they represent people (or animals etc.) in *general*.

images – things which are made (drawings, paintings or models, which represent an idea or a real object.

Impressionist – the name given to a group of painters who were interested in *capturing* a particular time of day or atmosphere.

print – a *reproduction* of an image from a flat plate or surface.

relief carving – shallow carving on a flat surface which makes the figure appear to stand out from the background

studies – drawings or sketches of things or people which are made to get information or to try out an idea before making the final object.

The publishers would like to thank the following for permission to reproduce photographs and other copyright material :

pp 2/3 *1 Bridgeman Art Library/Louvre, Paris; 2 National Gallery, Beggruen Collection; 3 National Portrait Gallery; 5 National Portrait Gallery, © David Ball;* **pp 4/5** *1 Memling Museum, Bruges; 2 Tate Gallery;* **pp 6/7** *1 Bridgeman Art Library/Private Collection; 2 Bridgeman Art Library/Private Collection; 3 The artist; 4 British Museum, Coins and Medals Collection;* **pp 8/9** *1 Bridgeman Art Library,/British Museum, London; 2 Michael Macintyre; 3 Oxfam/Ross Payne; 4 Art Council/Orissa State Museum, India;* **pp 10/11** *1 Editions Gaud; 2 Editions Gaud; 3 Groening Museum, Bruges/Cel Fotografie; 4 Greoninge Museum, Bruges/Cel Fotografie;* **pp 12/13** *3 Prado Museum, Madrid; 4 Tate Gallery; 5 Fitzwilliam Museum, Cambridge;* **pp 14/15** *1 Tate Gallery; 2 Royal Academy; 3 Tate Gallery © D Hockney 1977; 4 Tate Gallery © DACS 1994;* **pp 16/17** *1 Metropolitan Museum of Art, New York; 2 Oxfam/Carol Wills; 3 National Portrait Gallery; 4 Giraudon;* **pp 18/19** *1 Bridgeman Art Library/National Archeaological Museum, Athens; 2 National Portrait Gallery; 3 Victoria and Albert Museum; 4 Tate Gallery; 5 Réunion des Musées Nationaux, Paris;* **pp 20/21** *1 Bridgeman Art Library/Phillips Collection, Washington D.C.; 3 Courtauld Institute Galleries, London; 4 London Transport Museum,* © London Underground Ltd; **pp 22/23** *1 Knight of Glin, Glin Castle, Limerick; 2 National Museum of Art, Washington; 3 Tate Gallery;* **pp 24/25** *1 Bridgeman Art Library/Victoria and Albert Museum; 2 Galerie Rosengart, Lucerne/DACS, London; 3 Bridgeman Art Library/Christies. London © DACS 1994; 4 Bridgeman Art Library/Tretyakof Gallery, Moscow © ADAGP, Paris and DACS, London 1994;* **pp 26/27** *1 Victoria and Albert Museum; 2 British Museum; 3 British Museum; 4 Bridgeman Art Library/Prado, Madrid; 5 Bridgeman Art Library/Stadtische Kunsthalle, Mannheim;* **pp 28/29** *1 Bridgeman Art Library/Fransworth Museum, Maine; 2 Bridgeman Art Library/Museum of Modern Art, New York*

We would also like to thank **Jeff Tearle** and the pupils of **Frideswide Middle School, Oxford**, and **Michael Mayell** and pupils of **St. Philip and St. James First School, Oxford**, for help with the Things To Do Sections. The photography in the Things To Do Sections was by **Martin Sookias and Mike Dudley**.

Oxford University Press, Walton Street, Oxford OX2 6DP
© Oxford University Press

All rights reserved. First Published 1994. ISBN 0 19 834820 7
Printed in Hong Kong